Two
Gringos
in Brazil

Two Gringos in Brazil

A True Story So Scandalous it's Sick

MARK BURGOS

ARPress

ILLUMINATING IDEAS
EMPOWERING VOICES

ARPress
45 Dan Road Suite 5
Canton MA 02021

Hotline: 1(888) 821-0229
Fax: 1(508) 545-7580

Ordering Information:
Quantity sales. Special discounts are available on quantity purchases by corporations, associations, and others. For details, contact the publisher at the address above.

Printed in the United States of America.

ISBN-13: Softcover   979-8-89356-287-3
          eBook   979-8-89356-286-6

Library of Congress Control Number: 2024903324

A commercial if ya will..

NO MORE BALDING

My BROTHER is BALD, SUPPOSEDLY it's HEREDITARY is from your MOMS side of the family. My GRANDFATHER WAS BALD. BUT I am NOT going BALD!!! I purchased all kinds of CRAP from DIFFERENT companies. SPENDING a LOT of MONEY, MONEY I did NOT have, I HAVE been FIGHTING on GOING BALD ever since I was 25 years OLD, I'm 59 years OLD NOW I'm older than my BROTHER And my BROTHER IS BALD. I did NOT do THIS, but it would NOT HURT you by USING your favorite HAIR GROWING product, IF you feel BETTER by using them. I Did NOT use it, them. GROWING HAIR by USING a company's product WHILE you are going through my TECHNIQUE, it doesn't make SENSE. You DON'T need them. PLUS, you can SAVE A LOT of MONEY by NOT using them, but my TECHNIQUE, it WORKS!!! This IS what you DO. This worked for ME. I did it SEVERAL times day and NIGHT. It seems like it's PAIN in the ASS, but do you want to go BALD?!!! You DON'T need to keep on doing this, so much NEAR the END when your hair HAS GROWN IN. BUT You are ADDICTED by SQUEEZING your scalp, it doesn't hurt you, IT'S actually RECOMMENDED to do IT. I would USE my FINGERTIPS SQUEEZING my scalp INWARD on your HEAD. Like you're squeezing a TIT, the BREAST part of a WOMAN'S BODY the NIPPLE the AREOLA. All of that SEXY SOFTTITTY(..)

But DON'T SQUEEZE your head as SOFT as a BREAST!!!You WILL figure it out, how much pressure TO USE? I mean you don't wanna HURT your GIRLFRIEND or your WIFE or the CHICK you hit up on at the BAR that SWEET young THANG. You want to loosen your scalp the skin PART of your HEAD. You want the BLOOD FLOW going through your SCALP. You can FEEL it WORKING!!! Then after a few weeks LATER you take a COMB. NOW you're gonna THINK to yourself this guy is CRAZY ME!!! NO, YOU'RE NOT DOING THIS, you have been AVOIDING doing this. THIS whole TIME ever since you began to go BALD!!! You were AFRAID of the COMBS bristles IS PULLING your HAIR OUT. NO, it's NOT what you are doing, you use the FAT part of the COMB. You use bristles it's making the BLOOD flow RACE up your SCALP. You can FEEL it WORKING!!! By SCRAPING your SCALP, you use bristles the FAT part of the COMB. You WILL FEEL the BLOOD FEEDING your HAIR with my TECHNIQUE, it is WORKING.

!!! I'm 59 years old NOW. I'm a YOUNG MAN. I'm In THE PRIME of my LIFE!!! My TECHNIQUE may work FASTER on YOU a younger LAD. My INVENTION I could see in my MIRROR, I saw LIKE 7-9 months LATER on down the ROAD. You SEE I did NOT give UP!!! I did NOT see IT in my MIRROR, but you have to REALISE the HAIR on your HEAD. The HAIR is GONNA be MICROSCOPIC. Every month its GONNA GROW THICKER on your HEAD. YOU could get INSTANT RESULTS if you get it SURGICALLY INSTALLED!!! BUT My TECHNIQUE IS GOD'S WORK.

NO CHEMICALS, it's ALL NATURAL. I just FEEL GOD is USING my STORY. THERE IS a NATURAL WAY, now you think I MUST be a GENIUS or a ROCK SCIENTIST or something? NO I'm NOT, average GUY. You're reading words from a GUY that LOVES to get HIGH ON LIFE, FAST CARS, BEAUTIFUL WOMEN WITH A HARD BODY, BIG TITS, BEAUTIFUL PUSSY (SHAVED) I LOVE BEER, VODKA, RUM, ALL HARD ALCOHOL, I LOVE GETTING HEAD, I LOVE JIZZING ALL OVER HER, A GIRL'S FACE I LOVE SMOKING POT THROUGH a BONG. FUCK that JOINT SHIT, I would resort to this ONLY in a PINCH. I could keep on going But you the GIST!!! I AM YOUR AVERAGE GUY!!! I Am a FINAGLER or WHAT!!! You're Welcome.

THE BEGINNING OF
TWO GRINGOS IN BRAZIL

I was l in California living at LINCOLN MALIBU MEADOWS APTS working as a deck waiter at GLADSTONES PCH. I moved to MALIBU CYN APTS and my friends in California told me that I could pull it off in JAPAN. They are a very short POPULATION in JAPAN, and I could work there in JAPAN as a MODEL. I'm only 5,11 too short for the CALIFORNIA market. I could pull it off in JAPAN. I often say in the book MODEL, this and MODEL that, and you're gonna say to yourself this GUY is full of shit. I'm just telling you what happened to me. This book has its highs and lows. In the long run it makes sense of it all. Do you wanna know what's best about this book? I have pictures backing up my story. I'm telling you the TRUTH NO BULLSHIT. Do not JUDGE me, it's NOT the kind of book that tells you a LIE, it tells you the TRUTH no BULLSHIT. Before all of this, I was living in the MALIBU canyon apartments. I SURFED and worked in CALIFORNIA, and I was friends with a bunch of guys that SURFED and MODELD. and my friends would tell me of all the TRAVELING and ALL the GIRLS that were there.

I have never been to another COUNTRY before and I was amazed by my friends and their stories. And all of these guys were tall and good-looking guys. They would tell me about MILAN ITALY, GERMANY, ENGLAND, JAPAN, BRAZIL and I would go with them to their MODELING castings, and I looked at the other MODELS that were there. and I said to myself, I can do this SHIT no problem and I planned my ATACK on giving it a try. And my friends had a lot of friends that lived near me, and I became FRIENDS with all of them and they all SURFED and one of these GUYS did hair and makeup and photography for a living that lived near me. His name was JIMMY Jordan JJ for short. And I wanted to try modeling out and my friend Steven Lippman was a good photographer, as well as a MODEL SURFER and ALL of the MODELING magazine companies wanted tall good-looking people in the U.S.A so I Tried for JAPAN.

They were a short population in Japan. I was only 5"11 tall in the modeling business, in the U.S.A, they wanted at least 6"0 or tall or taller and all the modeling castings wanted to see your work experience that's what your modeling book is for; they want to see all of your experience. OK I had NO experience, but my friends wanted to help me out and make a modeling book. My friend RODNEY ROWLAND was going out with a model named TATIANA PETITS. She was VERY COOL and FAMOUS at this time. So, I asked her if she would help me out and take a picture with me. and I didn't know what to do for the picture and she knew THIS. She was very nice to me and showed me what to do for the picture. So, after the shoot, I drove to the camera shop and had it blown up 8 x 10 and I placed it in my book. My friends shot the rest of my book. They made my book look like it was all TEARSHEETS.

That's what they call, a picture torn out of a magazine, a TEAR SHEET in the MODEL WORLD. My friends shot the rest of my book. I had that ONE picture of me with that FAMOUS MODEL. So, it looks like I knew what I was doing as far as being a MODEL. My friends lent me a MODELING BOOK with a big logo on the front of the book saying the name of the AGENCY you were with. I was NOT tall enough or that good looking of a guy for OMRS MEN'S AGENCY in CALIFORNIA. But I told OMAR my plan of trying MODELING out. I was a DECENT looking guy but not that good looking of GUY for OMARS MEN'S AGENCY, but OMAR wanted to help me one day. OMAR called me saying that CINQ DEUX UN wants me to go to Japan.

They will pay for my plane ticket to get there. I will have to stay in Japan for 2 months. I will have an apartment with another MODEL then I called mom and all my friends telling them my plan worked out. I had to go to the CONSULATE and get a VISA and get a PASSPORT and that was a pain in the ASS. I didn't get any sleep the night before. I was soooooooooooooo nervous that night. The next morning my MOM and DAD and my DAUGHTER drove me to the AIRPORT. I'm on the PLANE now thinking of how JAPAN will be. It was a long ass PLANE flight getting there. When you first get to JAPAN, it's a different culture than AMERICAS all together, but it was so cool at the same time. I get to my apartment and check everything out. I got an apartment with no one there. I didn't have to share my apartment with another MODEL, I was lucky, I guess. I'm sure that picture with TATIANA help me out, getting an apartment by myself all the other models apartments were down the hall from me. They were packet like sardines, and I became friends with them. I partied with them and drank lots of BEERS. My neighbors would tell me of their time in JAPAN.

The next day I go with them to the AGENCY. The ladies that work there say hi MARKY SON, and to the MODEL next to me hello DANIEL SON my neighbor friend. Then a lady from your agency takes all the male models to their castings that were going on that day. Then she says to me, "Do you like your apartment MARKY SON?" and I say, "Oh just fine MAM". There were 5 other GUY MODELS with me. And at night we would go to all these FREE food and drink bars, there were many of them when you first got there. They would give you all these FREE drink and food tickets. When you run out of drink tickets just go to another free food and drink joint. There were many of them and the MODELS would bring in all the Japanese people with money and they would spend all of their money in their club, That's smart. We didn't care how they were USING US WE drank for FREE.

The drinking and clubbing didn't last long because you had to look GOOD for possible jobs. OK I'm lying to you, we partied all the time. I still couldn't believe that I was living like a CELEBRITY from my LOOKS. I have to thank GOD for my parents. This was all fun, it blew away painting houses at home. The next day, you have to take the SUBWAYS and walk our ASSES off to MODELING castings. The girl MODELS would have their own castings to go on. The guy MODELS would be trading their books showing all the work they have done.

Telling jokes and laughing. They all thought I was a BIG MODEL because of that picture with TATIANA but I didn't tell anyone it was FAKE. That picture was of my buddy RODNEY'S girlfriend. they all thought it was a TEAR SHEET, but I didn't tell anyone it was all FAKE.

The jobs I got were like sears-kmart- Target. Then I got my first commercial it was in OKINAWA ISLAND, a very pretty part of JAPAN. That island, the U.S.A BOMBED in World War 2 after JAPAN bombed pearl harbor HAWAII, your average model would NEVER bring a camera on a job. I'm sure, did I wanted pictures of my timer in JAPAN? you only live ONCE right? They even had a water-skiing boat. I will show you the pictures and the GIRL they picked for the job that was to be my WIFE. It was a big EGO BOOSTER for me. That car company had spent a lot of money and they hired ME for the job. I came home with 10 thousand dollars CASH in JAPANESE yen. I thought I was RICH, I never had that much MONEY before. The girl MODELS made a hell of a lot more MONEY than I did. I wasted that MONEY in no time. When you were in JAPAN you had the option to stay longer if you were working WHICH I WAS, but I wanted to go back and tell my stories to everyone. I was home for a couple years I never tried to MODEL in the U.S.A. I wasn't DUMB, I wasn't in the U.S.A MODEL league, plus you had to DRIVE lots of miles and WAIST lots of time and money and gas for NOTHING. They weren't going to pick ME. Turn the page, I'll let the pictures do the talking of my time in JAPAN.

My buddy JAIME STEIN was in BRAZIL MODELING, and I called him JAIME STEINLAGER because we drank lots LAGER together and we would SMOKED the GREEN da kine bra. When he was in town, JAIME and I were good friends from SURFING a lot together. Jaime came to my house one day with a friend named IVAN BERTAZO from BRAZIL and we went SURFING at MALIBU beach that day. And in the water, IVAN says to me, "I could model and stay at his family's house." IVAN was in business with his father making paintball products and they have a HUGE BOAT and IVANS friends have a water SKI BOAT. And on the weekends, we could water ski or SURF, so I want to go to BRAZIL for sure now. I was sick and tired of painting houses and my everyday lifestyle in CALIFORNIA. And I wanted to go because MODELING in JAPAN was so much fun. We went home from SURFING that night. I was talking to my friend JIMMY JORDAN on the phone, and I told him MY PLAN.

I was going to BRAZIL to MODEL JIMMY did hair and makeup and photography for a living. Ivan's girlfriend Andra was a HUGE MODELI in BRAZIL and she was represented by a huge modeling agency named FORD modeling agency. So, we set up a day to go to BRAZII with ME and JIMMY and like before I got no sleep thinking about it At the AIRPORT. I said goodbye to my family and my DAUGHTER. I gave a kiss to my MOM and DAUGHTER. I'm on the plane now and it was a long ass plane flight getting there. We got picked up by IVAN and his FATHER so now we're driving to Ivan's house the next morning. Ivan and his family have a maid that works there at the house, and she cooks us up a very scrumptious breakfast Brazil style meal. OK first of all Ivan says to me and jimmy you don't speak BRASIL with a Z we say it with a S BraSil its pronounced BRASSSSSSSSSIL they speak Portuguese in BRASIL and Ivan says to us jokingly you stupid GRINGOS say Portuguese with a Z in brasil we say it with a S its pronounced PORTUGESSSSSSSSSSSE egzagerted of course. Ivan and his girlfriend ANDRA drive us to meet the FORD modeling agency.

The ladies from FORD say to us "Let us see your work, meaning your books" they decided to take me on because of ANDHRA I'm sure and they take JIMMY because his workbook was outstanding looking. Some of the ladies speak good English and WE picked up on some of the Portuguese language. I got to remember saying BRASLI with a S we spoke with CALIFORNIA swagger and I liked to show off to the BRAZILIANS my ability to speak English well, well on the FLY ya know what I'm talkin about, we chose to speak in English and Portuguese and they loved to speak with me. They all said elles (they) fala (talk) Portu-Englese. The Portuguese we picked up on was sorta, ok I guess because you had their full attention well, I was in BRASIL MODELING and SURFING again with IVAN and the SURFERS in BRASIL were very competitive with ME.

Being a CALIFORNIA SURFER, I didn't hold back at all. I showed them what a CALIFORNIA SURFER was all about in time, I had their respect. Then a guy rolled up a JOINT and we smoked it :) and we went home all BAKED out of our minds. We ate some dinner, then it was time to go to the club to allure. The MUSIC was PUMPING there. THERE were so many BEAUTIFUL GIRLS there, it was SICK and they dance half NAKED sweating and glistening in the light (I) with TIGHT jeans on, it was FUCKIN MAGIC. I tell ya it was AMAZING. I worked a bunch. I did a bunch of magazines lay out work. They were working the SHIT out of jimmy so much he needed a VACATION. Soon it was time to get back to the USA are visas were going to expire plus I missed my daughter and my family. I started painting houses again and I hated it. My friend Jim Hartman came to my house one day and the guy invented the SWATCH guard for SWATCH watches. It was like a plastic rubber band for SWATCH watches and the guy made MILLIONS of dollars. My friend ERIC RECTOR came over to my house one day with his dog. He was a model himself and he helped me get going in the MODELING business.

ERIC and his wife SUSAN were breeding his dog. It was called a JAPANESE SHIBA dog, and he gave me one of the puppies and I got one of those FLEXI retractable dog leashes. And the only thing wrong with the leash was, there was no way of locking up your dog without having your companion help you. That's if you had a friend or companion with you to help. If you're by yourself, you're screwed. So, I invented a holder for the FLEXI. It was like a SURF leash with a circular rope at the end of the Velcro and nylon strap. You would put the Velcro part of it with the circular rope through the flexi hand handle, you pull it tight making the flexi swing around from a tree branch, or pole or whatever you attach it to, and the dog can go wherever it wants. But you have to come back relatively soon. In case your dog wraps itself around something. I went to a dog convention, and I talked to the owner of FLEXI. He liked my idea at first, then he said I will talk to you later on. Then I went home all excited and then I called him the next day and he says to me, "People will attach it to their wrist and the dog will run around a car or something and KILL them and they will SUE him" what a bunch of BULL SHIT all you need to say on the packaging. Don't attach it to your wrist or your body and wall you're not responsible, "But NO" he says, "I just think he doesn't want anybody making any MONEY from his product. So was all bummed for a bit then I loaded the BONG :)

One day I was hanging out at my friend TYLER'S house. He lived in the middle of MALIBU canyon in Montecito CALIFORNIA.

TYLER was playing around with my dog's leash one day and he says to me, "If you had 4 of these leashes you could tie up your girlfriend or wife to the bed, it would be great for the sex bondage business." and I thought to myself Tyler maybe on to something here and I thought if you sewed the Velcro on to a nylon strap you could strap up your chick to your each corner of the bed or we can make handcuffs then we said let's go........................ SURFING...................................and think more about our idea in the water.

The next day, we go and buy an industrial sewing machine through the recycler, and we go to the sports chalet store and buy nylon straps and Velcro and nylon straps so you could wrap it around a bed post or something. And at this time, I got kicked out of the malibu canyon apartments then I moved into Tyler's, mom's house, his mom was so cool, and she let me move in. We set up shop at Tyler's house then we drove to the nearest sex shop, and it was in Canoga park 15 minutes away from my parents' house and we go in the shop and look at their wide variety of sex toys products and we found the big sex toy manufacturer and distributer that was near us, and it was 45 minutes away in north Hollywood it was called Doc Johnson.

Called Doc Johnson and talked to their new product manager and his was Ron McAlister. So, we set up a meeting with Ron and we get dressed up in suits like we're smart businessmen--- yeah RIGHT we are. So, we drive down there in Tyler's beat up 69 ford mustang and we walk into Doc Johnsons and meet with Ron, so we go into his office and I start the meeting and we pull out our leashes and right away Ron loves are idea and right then, Ron thinks of a whole line of products with OUR idea, you could make a hooded cover and thigh cuffs and waist belt and right away we see dollar signs running through our heads and Ron says Doc Johnson sells their products WORLDWIDE, Ron ends the meeting.

Then we meet the owner of Doc Johnson and shake his hands and we go home and on the way home TYLER and MY smiles on our faces are so WIDE :) and we're so proud of ourselves. Then Tyler reaches behind him and pulls out the BONG. By the way did I ever tell you that me, Tyler and my friends are HUGE pot smokers of the GREEN, the GREENER the better, then we drive in bumper-to-bumper traffic all baked out of our minds :) then we crank up the radio and load the BONG and we smoke it. We LOADED it up with GREEN SAPPY BUD :) and at this time, the San Fernando valley was packed with TRAFFIC, but we didn't care how bad the traffic was, we were soooooooooooooooooooooooooo HIGH :)

We got home and we call everyone saying that we're so excited telling them that we are going to be RICH :) then I thought of Ivan and his father that they make plastic injection parts for his company, the paintball company. Once we got home, I called Ivan and asked him if he and his dad could make the plastic clip Ron was talking about and they said "YES we can". BRAZIL is a 3rd world country. So, making it there, it's gonna be cheaper than the U.S. Then we call Ron at Doc Johnson telling him that BRASILI is going to make the mold for us and that we were going to need money to make the mold and Ron says yes to us. We need to find that interchangeable CLIP that Ron was talking about.

Then we drove to the sports chalet sports chalet store, and we found the plastic clip Ron was talking about and that clip would make the bondage interchangeable, we could make all of the products in BRASIL and out of all my friends Tyler was considered my BEST friend. We had one thing in common we SURFED, and we had BIG dreams. When I was talking to Ivan, I explained to him the whole game plan that we struck GOLD with Doc Johnson, and we sold our idea to Doc Johnson and that we are going to make our idea in Brazil and that Doc Johnson will come down and meet us. I give the phone to TYLER, and he says to IVAN "He can't wait to meet him". When I lived at the Brazos house with JIMMY, Ivan and his family. Mr. Bertazzo was a very cool and smart businessman. Their boat was docked at Guaduja marina, it's a 2-hour drive from Sao Paulo. ME and TYLER started to get ready to go to BRASIL now. Doc Johnson gave us money to get the mold going. Tyler says goodbye to his family. My dad and mom and daughter take us to the airport, I kiss my daughter and mom goodbye. We are on the plane now so excited we're going to BRASIL; we land and get picked up by Ivan we drive to Ivan's house.

Tyler meets Mr. Bertazzo and they talk for a bit, then it's dinner time and the maid makes the family a BEAUTIFUL BRASILIAN MEAL. Then we get ready to go to the club allure we go in, and the music is PUMPIN'. perfect GOLDEN-BROWN ASSES are dancing

EVERYWHERE. I'm used to it. I've been to club allure before, and you should have seen TYLERS and MY face smiles from EAR to EAR:). We had a great time and that night, I was talking to IVAN'S friends telling them about our sex toy company invention and they were ROLLING with laughter. Then we go home and wake up and get ready for the day. We drink coffee and eat a perfect BRASILIAN STYLE MEAL. Then we go to ANDRAS MODELING AGENCY called FORD. We were in BRASIL to make are BONDAGE invention we MODELD for EXTRA MONEY. The FORD agency meets TYLER for the first time. It was MY AGENCY since the last time I was there. They look at TYLER'S book and sign him in right away. Then we went to IVAN'S business. TYLER meets everyone there at IVAN'S shop. Then it's time, we go meet are POT dealer :) you know the GREEN SHIT, but it wasn't GREEN though it was sorta BROWN looking. We load the BONG to try it out then BZZZZZZZZZZZZZZZ you see if your caught by the police in BRASIL with drugs, your fuct unless you pay them off.

Then we paid the DEALER for dirt BROWN BUD, but we didn't care if it was BROWN, it was BRASIL. Ok let me tell you what it's like to meet a GIRL for the first time. It doesn't matter how long you have KNOWN them or how BEAUTIFUL they are, they'll HUG you and KISS you :) from cheek to CHEECK to CHEEK it doesn't matter how BIG their TITS are :) (. .) they press them against you, ITS BEAUTIFUL I TELLI ya. :) then we go to IVANS business. We take are CLIP with us and show the tool maker guy the CLIP and he says to us "I will start making the mold for the CLIP and we went home to the bertazos house. It was a 4-bedroom house. It was tight but we worked it out." The tool guy was a smart businessman. I forgot his name. All I know is he was GERMAN. One day after working on the mold, it was time to go back to WHATERSKIING again. They have big rocks in the Guaduja ocean, and we drove the boat next to the rocks and we climbed up the rocks and jumped off them and into the ocean. It was fun. It rains in BRASILI like 3 times a day and the runoff from the rain goes into the jungle and then it goes into the ocean turning it green color.

The BRASLIAN dollar was a lower value than the AMERICAN dollar, so is AMERICAN dollar went a long way. We bought everything there, we even bought new SURFBOARDS. We located a BIG SURF industry, and it was called HANGLOOSE. In CALIFORNIA I SURFED with my friend STEVEN LIPPMAN and he was SPONSORED by big SURF industries and he gave me his old surfboards they were 6.1 - 6.2-inches long he gave me boards that he didn't want anymore. So, we got BIGGER SURFBOARDS in BRASIL for HUGE WAVES, the WAVES WEREN'T BIGGER than the U.S.A just more consistent where we were. It was BIG SURF where we were. The LONGER your BOARD, the BIGGER the WAVE. So, I got a 6.8 rounded end, tri fin thruster SURFBOARD and Tyler got a 6.10 pin, tri fin thruster SURFBOARD we got it from HANGLOOSE.

The BRASILIAN girls were AMAZING looking and being AMERICAN it was like being a CELEBRITY just because you were AMERICAN, and they all loved to speak English with US. They were intrigued with US, and they wanted to talk with US, and we loved their UNDIVIDED ATTENTION. They liked calling us GRINGOS, we didn't mind the BRASILIAN girls AREN'T SLUTS they most likely had boyfriends. They just wanted to know more about you. They said to us why are you here when I told them, we're here to MODEL and make are INVENTION with Ivan, just not something you hear every day in Brasil. Then we said we were from MALIBU, CALIFORNIA. It was just not something you hear every day in BRASIL, and everybody has heard of MALIBU.

So, we became fast friends with everyone. IVAN was with at the taxi modeling agency. One night at club allure we ran into this guy named MARCUS PANTHERA. He was one of the owners of a taxi modeling agency. We were talking to him, and he said to us "We could model with his agency" and he said, "I have a beach house at CAMBURI beach, and I go to it every weekend and you guys could stay at his beach house with us. And we could SURF and SMOKE MACOINYA that's what a BRASILIAN people calls POT MACOINYA" and we sat back for a bit and we said to ourselves sure why not, "OK, first of all you don't ever think about leaving an agency like FORD to go to a small agency like taxi but we weren't in BRASILI to model, we went to BRASIL cause of are INVENTION but FORD could care less if I left, I was too short, plus none of them had a beach house we could stay at and some of the GIRL MODELS from taxi MODELING was there so we BAILED FORD and said HELLO taxi."

Some of the MODELS lived near ME and TYLER but we had IVAN to bring us to MARCUS BEACH house. What would you rather do? go to MARCUSES by IVAN or have BEAUTIFUL GIRL MODELS take you there? :) At this time, there were BIG beer company parties going on and ALL the MODELING AGENCIES were invited to GO to the PARTIES, and we knew all of the MODELS that were there and we PARTIED for FREE. I told you the book was GOOD. Some time passed one day I was doing a BEACH foot thong commercial with IVAN and kids and other MODELS were there. We filmed it at one of the local SURF breaks at MARESIAS BEACH and I knew a guy there that had a BOAT.

I told the DIRECTOR I could BAREFOOT waterski, so they decided to put their BEACH thongs on my feet and I BAREFOOT waterskiing with the thongs on my feet where the water was CALM early in the morning. Then Some time passes, and there was a GIRL named KELLI CHRISTIE from a taxi MODELING AGENCY and TYLER knew her. It was a tight living at IVANS place. So, we moved into KELLY CHRISTIE'S place. SHE was an artist, and she was a great COOK, and HER house was BEAUTIFUL, and she smoked the GREEN. Well, you know what I mean. You had to take the SUBWAY to get to Kelly's house.

MARCUS PANTHERA had his own MODELING AGENCY called GUNS, he left taxi and the WORLD CUP was going on.. and all of the MODELING AGENCIES were INVITED to go to them was a SOCCER player named HOMARIO he was really good and when BRASIL would SCORE against the UNITED STATES, the BRAZILIAN people would look at ME and TYLER, but we CHEERED for the BRASILAN.

"TEAM we were in BRASIL it was time to go home the BRASIL TEAM, WON the WORLD CUP we got home and eat KELLY makes us a wonderful BRASILIAN meal."

I wish I could tell you I was a big STUD!!!

I was looking through a GQ magazine and I thought I could copy this guy's pose and I went to a department store called BULLOCKS WILSHIRE in woodland hills California and I bought a GEORGIO ARMANI black suit, and I had my BUDDIES shoot the picture. Then I developed it. I picked out the best picture and I had it blown up 8x10. I got a GIORGIO ARMANI logo out of a GQ magazine and glued it under MY picture. I took it over to KINKOS and got it laser copied 8X10 and WALA INSTANT TEAR SHEET:) that's what they call a picture torn out of a magazine in the modeling WORLD. BRASIL would never know the DIFFERENCE. I could say I shot in California. BRASIL wouldn't think TWICE about it plus I was a SURFER from AMERICA just not something you hear every day in BRASIL, and they all thought I was the GIORGIO ARMANI GUY and that pic with TATIANA PETITS I was only 5"11 and NOT a drop dead good looking guy. So WHY was considered a BIG model because I convinced them. I WAS just BULLSHIT, and I got a lot of work from that supposed TEAR SHEET. So here is this guy ME!!! That started modeling from BULLSHIT and I'm still BULLSHITING when is the BULLSHIT EVER gonna STOP? :)-

START

Brazil has the worst AIDS epidemic in the WORLD, and you should have seen me and Tyler with all these SEXY WOMAN!!! and you thought to yourselves, YAAAH these guys are getting laid left and right. NO not at alL... The girls most likely have boyfriends, and they aren't SLUTS, they just wanted to know more about you... and we were big showoffs to them, and it doesn't matter how long you have known them... When they first see you... a girl hugs and kisses you and we were like BRING IT ON and we loved it THERE. The people in Brazil have pure hearts!!! Kelly christie, TYLER'S GIRLFRIEND always went to RIO DE JANEIRO KL during CARNIVAL every year, and she has a guy friend who lives there in RIO because ALL of BRASIL celebrates CARNIVAL.

It is Sooooooooooooooooo FUCKIN BITCHEN in RIO DE JANERO. I'll shut up NOW and let all the pictures do all the talking. MY buddy from Australia named Rolf. They couldn't pronounce R that was weird cause in BRASIL is pronounced with an R instead of pronouncing Rolf they called him HOFF, Rolf was a MODEL SURFING pot smoking AUSTRALIAN himself and they couldn't pronounce steven correctly instead of saying ST, they called him SCHTEVEN and TYLER accepted it that way. And they couldn't pronounce TYLER Correctly, there was no WAY I was gonna call him CORECTLY SO I called him TAYLOR. His full name was, Steven Tyler Stobie, and that famous singers name was steven Tyler, Tyler had everyone in California call him Tyler instead of calling him Steven.

For some weird reason, I would have stayed with my original name in time we became good friends with Rolf (HOFF) he was a local at Maresias beach. Ok look at the picture, you see the first 2 red lines? it was right in that middle of those 2 red lines it was thick JUNGLE BUSH in that picture.... and Me and Tyler's shed, are beach house, there was a river alongside it we SURFED in front of Myra's house all RIGHT breaking WAVES and we had SHIT bikes to ride round. Plus, it was way cool to ride them around breathing Beach air and sun going through your body AND SOOOOOOOOOOOOOOOOOOOOOOOOOOOOOOO HIGH it was FUCKIN MAGIC! I TELL YA!!! Some time passed and ME and TYLER MOVED TO CAMBURI BEACH we were at Marcus beach house with Marcus for 1 1/2 weeks. We were renting a beach house near Panthera's beach house, then ME and TYLER have our friend from the U S A named ERIC RECTOR. Who came to BRASIL to see what me and TYLER have been talking about all of these years.

We were smoking MAKKOINYA da GREEN and ERIC was the KING of smoking pot ME and TYLER made a BONG out of BAMBOO, and we put in a down tube and INSTANT BONG. The BRASILIAN people were amazed at this device. They only smoked joints in BRASIL I guess that's what you get from a 3rd world country. My girlfriend VANNESA went home earlier but ERIC had just got to BRASIL, but we wanted to show ERIC more of BRASIL. There was a girl from taxi MODELING agency named PATRICIA MARIA. She was HOT looking with BIG ol vacuum machine lips she looked like she could suck the chrome off a TRAILER HITCH, and she asked me if she could smoke a BONG with ME, so I said it's in my room. So, I took her back to my room and she sat on my bed and then after SMOKING the MACOINYA that's not the only thing she WHIPPED out, she unzips my pants and starts sucking my COCK. Ok I'm not gonna lie to ya. I was already HARD, she was shaking her ASS and TEASING the shit out of me. TYLER was going out with her FIRST BUT we both knew HER from our agency, one night after going to club allure, me and her hooked up and I PLOWED her for a while, but I felt like shit doing that to VANESSA after that, she became TYLER'S GIRLFRIEND me and TYLER called her the JUICER. she had LIPS like a human vacuum machine.

We had to get back our things to go home to Sao Paulo. MARCUS'S nephew ARMANDO and his friend BILL were going back to Sao Paulo. We asked them if we can get a ride home with them and they said "Sure come on." We pack things and put them in the car. Most of the people in BRAZIL are celebrating Christmas and the new year holiday at the beach and they went back to Sao Paulo when VANNESA went HOME, but some of the people stayed longer as we did. They drove like there in the Indianapolis 500 so fast and dangerous and most of them are drunk out of their minds and driving home and there was a drunk old man driving home. He hits us in the back of the car and sends us flying through the JUNGLE.

Ok here is when the story even gets WORSE. TYLER flies out of the window and hits his HEAD and BREAKS his NECK and DIES

INSTANTLY. We didn't have are SEAT BELTS ON. I was FUCKED up and couldn't BREATHE. I broke my RIBS and tore up my insides and punctured a LUNG, and was BLEEDING and there were DOCTORS and a couple CARS back of our car. They saw the CRASH luckily, they had their MEDICAL BAGS with them IN THE JUNGLE? Was I lucky or WHAT!!! I was in the JUNGLE.... the DOCTOR helped me BREATH AGAIN IN THE FUCKIN JUNGLE I have TO thank GOD!!! Was GOD on my side or what?! Well, the doctor he helped me, BREATH again...some of the people came over to STEAL what they could, luckily the people got the POT. Thank GOD!!! cause if you're CAUGHT in brasil with drugs your fuckt. Unless you PAY THEM OFF and ERIC can't speak Portuguese and defend me now. The police arrived and they took me to a local hospital. It was a 3rd world hospital, and they can only do so much, and they say in the crash I only have a 10 percent chance of living..

Some people at the crash accident took Eric in a car with them. They can't understand ERIC. NOTHING happened to Bill, Armando Eric just scraped his face. Bill and Armando can't speak English either. Eric must have been freaking out when his good buddy died. His other friend is on the edge of dying and coughing up blood and in a coma. Armando was Marcus's nephew, so he calls Marcus on his cell phone and tells him what happened and where we are. Marcus grabs his friend Guilherme and they hall ass where we are. Now it's 2 1/2 hours after the crash. There were police at the hospital, and they asked Marcus what happened and Guillerme, "Are you friends with the dead guy?" Marcus first runs into his nephew Armando and his friend Bill, and they are explaining to him what happened then Marcus finds Eric and now Eric is so relieved he had someone that understood him.

Eric tells Marcus what happened and now Marcus has to identify Tyler's body and they left Tyler in the car and Marcus gets infuriated with the old man who hit us wanting to kill the guy. This whole time Guillerme was trying to find a helicopter company to fly me to Sao Paulo, she FOUND one and Eric is calling my DAD, Guillerme gets the credit card number from ERIC. Now, Guilherme calls the helicopter company and gives them the card number and they flew me over to the hospital to fix me up. Now Marcus and Guilherme drove to Sao Paulo by the hospital where the man who hit us parked their car. They went to the hospital; they find his room. Marcus starts to yell at the man. The man is acting like he could care less. Marcus' friend died and his other friend is dying. He starts yelling at the man and put his hands around his neck. The man's family were there and stopped Marcus. The hospital police arrived and found out what happened, and they let Marcus go. The next day I was shipped to a hospital in Sao Paulo. I was still in a coma and that night my parents arrived.

Vanessa drives my parents to the hospital. A couple of days later, I'm in California in a hospital still in a coma. I woke up after2 '/ months. Then I got released from the hospital...

Vanessa had to go home, and her visa was up. Like 3 months later me and Vanessa BROKE UP!!! over the phone. OK let me tell you what it's been like living my life. I could get ready to go to the bathroom not holding on to anything or anybody then I got an electric scooter I used it for years. I would use it in my 24-hour gym. Then I got a bicycle. A tricycle way easier to use my balance still sucks to this day. I drove my scooter like a mad man in my gym. I had no patience then I got a 3-wheel tricycle my balance still sucks. The bike has a basket in the back of this bike. It's like A truck. It's way faster than the scooter and I ride it everywhere I carry all kinds of crap from the market. It's been years since the accident every day. It is a wonder if I will meet the girl of my dreams. When I would talk with a girl, and I saw a chance with hooking up with her then I would scare them away.

I used to have more women than you could shake a stick at. I've had 3 jobs since the accident. I worked at Val surf when I lived at my parents' house. I was still recovering from the accident. My parents bought me a trailer and I moved into a trailer park near van Nuys California with my dog Zooky. I got a job at ralphs, I use to put store merchandise away for my job. I used access services to get around. I used my 3-wheel bicycle to get around. I used to take my dog for walks when I walked with her. My friends would come over and we smoked some GREEN if ya know what I mean. It was the U S A not BRAZIL some healthy big GREEN SAPPY BUD and some CORONA.

Ralphs was on SATICOY and BALBOA and there was a chicken Mexican burrito FOOD joint, and I was FRIENDS with the owner later on he passed away. I used to walk the park to practice my balance. Then my parents bought me a condo in WESTHILLS CALIFORNIA. When I worked at VAL SURF AND I would ride my bike to and from home. I used to have my SURF buddies come to my work and buy SURF shorts and wax with my discount. There was MISSION BURRITO and BOBBY'S coffee shop and my SIMON RHEE taekwondo. My buddy CHRIS CARNEL was a BLACK BELT we would SMOKE da GREEN if ya know what mean jellybean. The WOODLAKE bowl and Kennedy's SURF shop and my bank of AMERICA.

One day, my friend CHRIS CARNEL, came by and we got HIGH. He was reading my book and he said to me, "This is how you used to talk by reading my story." I have to thank GOD for the TV shows I like, FRIENDS I like Joey and Chandler, Ross has his moments of LAUGHTER, but he is such a kiss ASS for RACHEL penally. I'd love to kiss her ASS myself :) I used to have the playboy RACHEL was in and she looked HOT but that was years ago. GOD knows what she looks like now. I can't imagine bad because she is like my age NOW, wishful thinking on my end. I guess although like I said before, I'd love to kiss her Rear end ( ) like COUNTING CARS cause I used to have a 1967 Rs CAMARO. I had a big block 427 CHEVY race motor with ALUINUM HEADS in the car from my dad's parts store. I wrote this book years ago. I started it again cause I had nothing else to do................................

I worked at HOME DEPOT. I was in the garden department, and I took care of all the plants that were there. It looked SHARP when I was working, but their BATHROOM was so far far away. It was in a different GALAXY. So, I would go in a place that NO one saw, so I THOUGHT the MANAGER saw me PISSING in the palm tree BARREL and FIRED me on the SPOT. I was so bummed at that time. BUT my DAD said to me that I worked for a long time NOW, and you're not MARRIED, and you don't have a lot of BILLS, you can RETIRE now and have the GOVERNMENT pay your bills, that's what social security deductions in your paychecks are for. You probably will get some of that money back you won't live like a millionaire. But you could live a pretty frickin GOOD LIFE and we paid for your CONDO already and you don't have a WIFE nickel and diming you to DEATH. You can live pretty frickin good NOW and you should have seen the SMILE on my face from ear to ear. :)

My MOM and my DAD passed away at this time and I was really bummed for a while and as many years went by. Then I was at my gym, and I fell off the TREADMILL and broke my kneecap, and I still had my injuries from BRASIL on top of what I have now. I'm pretty TWEAKED NOW, I can't even walk, have to use my WHEELCHAIR now to get around. I went to the west hills HOSPITAL they fixed it sorta, I can't walk now and then I went to the west hills assisted living facility not far from my home. I used to drive by it all the time when I was in NORMAL CONDITION, and I would think nothing about it.

Little did I know I'd be LIVING there a super long time, unless I had my daughter. I don't have a WIFE or a family to take care of me and the GOVERNMENT wouldn't let me go home, even though I had a condo 1 1/2 miles away but no one to take care of me. I used to have a ZILLION FRIENDS. I guess, I chose the wrong ones in life. I can't expect that they're going to change their whole life for me. My brother and sister ain't worth a SHIT and my parents died. I had no one to rely on BOO HOO I GUESS on oh well I'm not gonna cry for anyone. My DAUGHTER lives in COLORADO now, so had my DAUGHTER find another assisted living home that's where I'm at now.

I'm typing my book from a computer they have at the assisted living home. I just PISSED in the trash can under the computer I'm typing on and got busted by one of the CNA nurses. I hope she doesn't say anything to anybody, I talk like chase the spaz. I write like I used to. I typed this whole book with one finger. I'm the ONE finger bandit. Guess what FINGER is used...?

Since I can't speak well, I'm writing my HUMMER on paper. It's better than me telling you the story. I talk like chase the spaz.

The End

HOW I LOST MY VIRGINITY

There was a house for sale 3 blocks away from my parent house. In the San Fernando Valley, Woodland Hills California, the street name ERWIN and WOODLAKE. I was 15 years old, were talking about my skateboard years. The house had a pool that was empty. This was when skateboard parks were popular, anyhow we skateboarded the empty pool. Word on the street was, there was an empty pool to skate. One day there was 3 girls that went to that house from are school. I knew them, they came over to watch boys skateboard, anyhow a girl liked me, and she flirted with me. So, we went to a room in the house, and we stated to make out. and guys you know the rubber in your pocket. A couple years old cause you NEVER used it, well today was its usage. I PLPOWED the underage girl and when we were done. I pulled the cum filled rubber off and threw it out the window. The next day me and a couple friends went to skate the pool, but as we went through the side gate to the pool, I saw a cum filled rubber dangling in the wind on the neighbor's side gate. I'm sorry but that's FUNNY !!! I can remember a kid that was there named Acheme Shotkowski, GOD his parents never gave him a shot.

We're talking the 5th grade at the Woodlake Elementary School at San Fernando Valley California. There was a mongoose dirt bike. In the bike racks, anyhow the bike had a cheap ass bike lock and my dad had tools to snap that lock. So one day I went to school and I went home early that day. So I could steal that bike but as I went to the bike rack, I saw a kid that came over to steal the same bike and he had his dad's tools like me. So we stole the same bike and we went to Greg's house and we parted it out. We took the pieces we wanted. GREG still is my friend today we're still friends from that predicament.

"Wake up and smell the coffee, GOD is saying QUIT saying GOD DAM IT"

I've decided to MAKE the BONDAGE business WORK for me, MINE AND TYLER'S INVENTION. I'm thinking of a name NOW, should I call it's STRAP UP YOUR CHICK TODAY or call it GRINGOS BONDAGE? GRINGOS BONDAGE.COM...TIE UP YOUR CHICK OR MAN TODAY!!!

Go ahead and order on the WEB........HELLO!! Can we help you!!! We accept VISA, MASTER CARD, AMERICAN EXPRESS, OR CASH ....ORDER TODAY.

You remember the DOG retractable leash holder. I'm thinking of making that work also. I'm thinking of a name for how about DOG BONDAGE.COM, STRAP UP YOUR DOG TODAY!!! GO AHEAD AND ORDER have your credit card HANDY.

This is MY technique for problem sleepers when you wake up 3-4 take a sleeping pill if you have one if not ok. You won't go back to sleep if you do PERFECT, I never did, I wish I did. If you wake up at 5 don't take the sleeping pill you could be tired for the day. Perhaps a Bongi the old WAKE and BAKE lay back in bed EYES SHUT1...in the MORNING.

Instead of walking back forth through your house. That's why you're so tired for the whole day drinking tons of coffee. all you NEED to do is STAY in bed turn the tv on. Turn down the volume leave lights off. Close your eyers, shut, LEAVE them shut. Concentrate to your favorite channel leave your eyes shut. That's the key leaving your eyes shut.

FOR PEOPLE IN A WHEELCHAIR LIKE ME. THEY HAVE NO IDEA ABOUT IT. ITS MY INVENTION. GO TO SUNNY, HEALTH, FITNESS WEBSITE. ORDER PORTABLE STANDING. I HAVE NO IDEA WHY THEY SAY STANDING. LOOK AT THE WEBSITE THE GIRL IS SITTING IN A CHAIR. LIKE YOUR WHEELCHAIR YOUR WELCOME.

Your thinking to yourself.

"Ok mark where is GOD now? When all of these people are dying in this HORRFIC WAR. GOD works in mysterious ways. GOD has a plan. It takes time and plans from GODLY people, just keep the FAITH."

NEVER SAY NEVER

MARK'S FAMILY PICTURE

"GOD DAM IT", my Dad's favorite words.

My Dad's favorite words was, god dam it. And I hated when he said that. It didn't make sense. One night, my family was eating dinner. My Dad's fork slip to the ground and he said, "God dam it" Finally, I couldn't hear it no more. Andi stood up and said loudly, "What the fuck did God do to deserve that?" and my mom started laughing.

So, every time he said that I would say in a harsher words, "What the fuck did God do to deserve that?" Finally, he quit

THE BONDAGE, OUR IDEA.

CAME FROM A SURFLEASH, MY SURFBOARD.

Top of our Game in Brasil

My old Trailer in Trailer Park Van Nuys, California. Next photo is my Jeep, Cherokee Chief 4x4. The Family Dog Cody Man, on the retrack table. Dog leash holder, on Jeep door handle working my invention, working picture proof, SO ORDER DOG HOLDER (DLH.com) DOG LEASH HOLDER order.

JAIME STEIN, LISA (hugging Jamie),
RODNEY ROWLAND IN MEXICO.

Tyler and Mark longboarding in 2nd Point Malibu.

Half Pipe Pictures

MY DAUGHTER KRYSTA

JEREMY GRANDKIDS

THINGS YOU SHOULD
KNOW
THAT PIC ON THE
FRONT? IT WAS 30
DEGREES. WE
COULDN'T FEEL OUR
TOES, BUT WE GOT
THE SHOT. OH, AND
WE LOOK THAT
EVERYDAY. WE
DIDN'T DO IT JUST
SPECIAL FOR A
CHRISTMAS CARD OR
ANYTHING SILLY
LIKE THAT.

JILL SMITH exclusively for tinyprints
www.shutterfly.com/tinyprints

MERRY CHRISTMAS FROM THE MACGRAY FAMILY | 2017

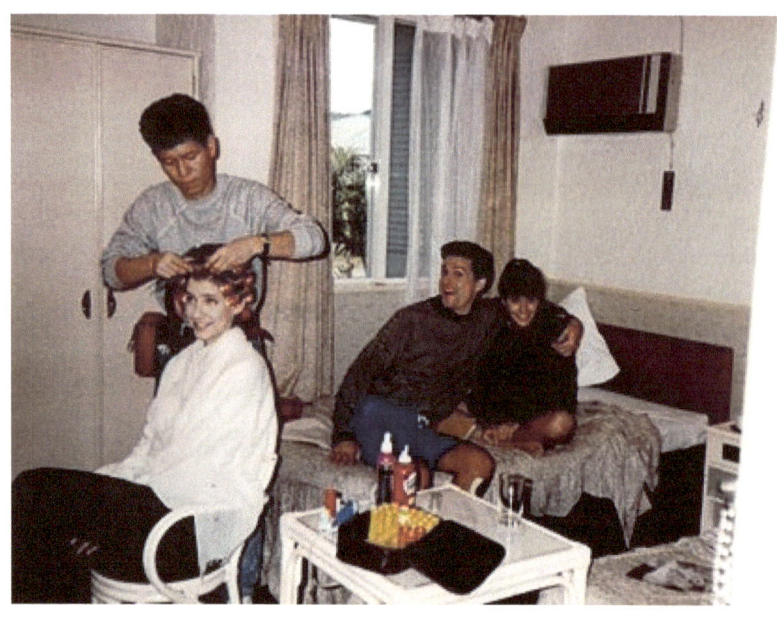

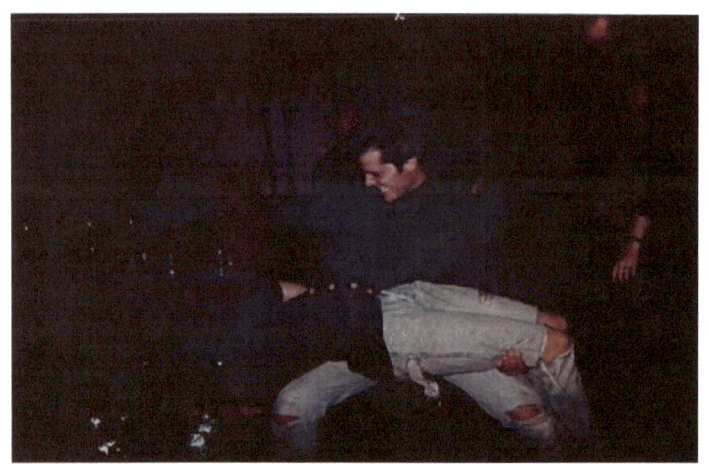

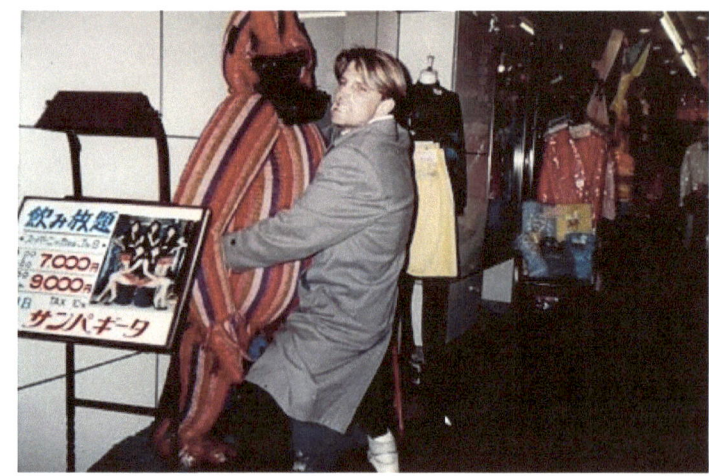

Height 167 Bust 86 Waist 60 Hips 88 Shoes 24 Hair Brown Eyes Brown

VANESSA VHOLKER

steve lipman, eric rector, Rodney Rowland.

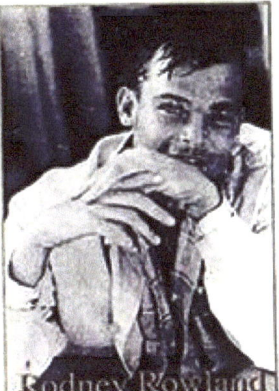

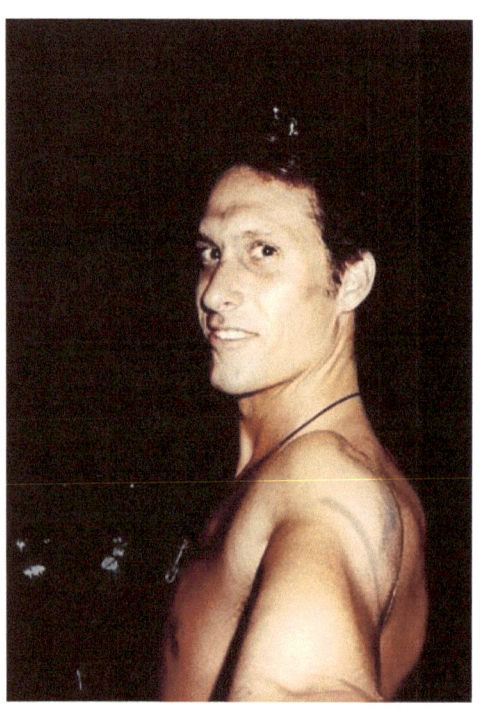